Art of Saints

A CELEBRATION OF HOLY MEN AND WOMEN

Sr Wendy Beckett

...lications

Published by **Redemptorist Publications**
Alphonsus House, Chawton, Hampshire, GU34 3HQ UK
Tel. +44 (0)1420 88222, Fax +44 (0)1420 88805
email rp@rpbooks.co.uk, www.rpbooks.co.uk
A Registered Charity limited by guarantee.
Registered in England 3261721.

Copyright © Redemptorist Publications 2011

First published as a series of *The Sunday Bulletin* from September to November 2010

First published in book form March 2011

Layout and cover design by Rosemarie Pink

ISBN 978-0-85231-385-5

A CIP catalogue record for this book is available from the British Library.

Printed by Lithgo Press Limited, Leicester, LE8 6NU.

Contents

Picture credits

This book is based on Sr Wendy Beckett's reflections originally published in Redemptorist Publications' *Sunday Bulletin* series from September to November 2010. It also includes a number of new reflections written especially for this volume.

It is a companion volume to Sr Wendy Beckett's *The Art of Faith*, *The Art of Christmas* and *The Art of Mary*, also published by Redemptorist Publications.

About the author

Sr Wendy is a well-known art historian, author and TV presenter. Born in South Africa in 1930, she joined the Sisters of Notre Dame when she was 16. She graduated from Oxford University in 1953 and returned to South Africa until 1970 when she moved back to England. She now lives as a hermit in the grounds of the Carmelite monastery at Quidenham, Norfolk.

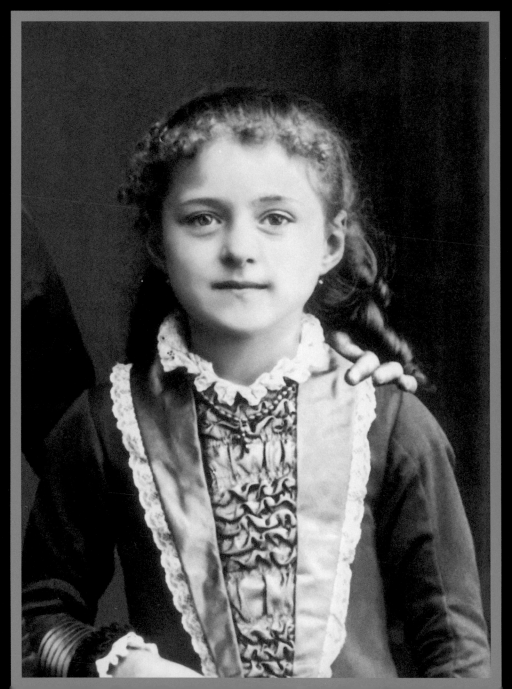

St Thérèse of Lisieux, 1873–1897

Photograph, 1881, Carmelite Monastery

Although there are many pictures of saints, few are actually portraits. Those saints who did have their portraits painted were mostly unfortunate in not attracting artists of much skill. The only exception that comes to mind is St Thomas More, who was painted by Holbein, though it was his position as statesman and celebrated intellectual that was being recorded, not so much his sanctity. Thérèse of Lisieux was painted quite often, mostly by her sister, and fellow Carmelite, Céline. But these works, however deep the love that prompted them, are hardly art.

Fortunately, Céline also took many photographs, and here we are in the unusual position of knowing in hard actuality what St Thérèse looked like. All agree that she was angelically pretty, an opinion not wholly borne out by the photographs. She is pretty, of course, with her big blue eyes and cascades of hair, but she has an overlong and very determined chin. It is the chin rather than the curls which gives us an insight into Thérèse. When we consider that she died when she was twenty-four, it seems to me that she was as much a genius, spiritually, as Mozart or Shakespeare.

The photograph I have chosen is not one of those Céline took inside the monastery. This one was taken by a professional photographer when Thérèse was eight. Her mother had died four years earlier and Thérèse was now the adored youngest of a family of six sisters. Both parents were devout Catholics, and all the girls became nuns, five of them Carmelites in Lisieux. Here we see Thérèse, dressed to the nines, ruffled and flounced, her hair an elaborate arrangement of ringlets. Her father, M. Martin, assuaged his grief over his wife's death by enshrining in his affections his "little queen". She was spoilt and pampered, not an easy child but one surrounded by constant love and admiration. She acknowledges herself how self-willed she was, and who could wonder at it?

When her two eldest sisters, Marie and Pauline, became Carmelites, fifteen-year-old Thérèse determined to follow them, despite clerical opposition. Her steely insistence brought her what she desired. This is hardly the recipe for a life of supreme holiness, yet Thérèse turned all its disadvantages – her privileged upbringing, her special status as community darling – into positive assets. All we need to become close to God is to desire it and to let God achieve it within us. This young teenager desired God with a passion that cut through all pretence.

The culture of her milieu made very much of physical penance: Thérèse, who so longed to be a saint, saw that the sisters most admired in the monastery were those who undertook the most severe penance. Here is where we see her genius. She could cut through all the romanticism and look straight to God. The Jesus that we see in the Gospels was uninterested in physical mortification. He never suggested that his followers should scourge themselves, and his attitude towards fasting raised not a few contemporary eyebrows. The life of Carmel was hard enough in itself. Thérèse saw that it was not necessary to look for suffering: the suffering was there for everybody, just in the daily course of living.

God did not ask for extraordinary deeds, God asked for love. Thérèse, instructed only by her own prayer, set herself on what she called her "Little Way". This meant that she did everything for love: the smallest thing – picking up a pin, smiling when she felt irritated, listening patiently to the boring tales of other sisters, not defending herself when her actions were misinterpreted. It sounds simple, and it is simple, but it is very far from easy. To lead a life wholly given to loving God in the small actualities of every day means a complete surrender of all selfishness and pride.

I have always been very moved by what she said about God's mercy. Everybody prays for mercy: Thérèse said that she expected as much from God's justice as from God's mercy. This was not at all because she felt that she was blameless, far from it. What she did feel was that blame, as well as praise, was God's business. Thérèse sought truth and she grasped, as very few have done, that it is only God who knows the complete truth. Neither family nor the closest of friends, nor we ourselves, really know the full truth of what we are and what we can be. The whole range of our weakness and of our strengths, the full weight of early experience, and what it has made of us, all these factors are known only to God. Of all the saints, I feel St Thérèse teaches us most surely about what it is to love.

St Bernadette, 1844–1879

Bernadette's Embroidery, 2008, by Greg Tricker,
Piano Nobile Gallery, London

One of the abiding fascinations of St Bernadette is that there is
so little to get hold of. It baffled her superiors in the convent,
and it baffles us today. She was in the paradoxical position of
receiving the sustained and admiring attention of millions,
while feeling herself to be of the utmost insignificance. In some
ways, hers was a peculiarly passive life. It was not what she did
but what was done to her, for her, that was of such universal
significance. We all know the story of Lourdes, and how this
little peasant girl, poor, malnourished (she was fourteen but
looked about eleven), sickly, uneducated, was visited one spring
morning by Our Blessed Lady. This astonishing event marked
her for ever as different.

Remember, the crowds who flocked to Lourdes, to see Bernadette
talking to the lady, saw nothing but Bernadette herself. There
was nothing whatever to prove that this was not a gigantic
hallucination: no gentle breezes, no glimmering light, nothing.
Yet Bernadette was herself her own authentication. The crowds

looked at this little creature, with her face upturned towards what she alone could see, and even the most cynical or sceptical were silenced. The visions came to an end, but what they had started never ended.

Bernadette could not see that this was anything to do with her. She gave as an example taking a broom from behind the door, sweeping with it; and then back behind the door it goes again. She saw herself as that broom: Our Lady had used her and put her away, and there was no credit owing to Bernadette herself. She suffered intensely from the continuing interest of pilgrims, putting up patiently, but with inner rebellion, with their intrusive questioning and the sound of their cameras. She desired with all her heart that what Our Lady wanted would come about: that there would be a church built in her honour and that people would pray the rosary. But having told the authorities, which for her meant her parish priest, she felt that it was now in safe hands. She treasured in her heart what had happened: she had no desire to speak about it, she had no desire to be noticed.

It is her life as a nun that most attracts me, especially since one feels that she only became a nun because it seemed the best thing to do. It protected her privacy. The nuns were both deeply impressed to have the "visionary" come among them and even more deeply taken aback by how ordinary she was. She was a person no one would notice.

Greg Tricker has noticed her, has understood with his own unique sensitivity the humble innocence of this young woman. He has sculpted, painted, drawn and etched images that show all the aspects of her life. *Bernadette's Embroidery* shows her nearing the end. What we see here is the seriousness of her concentration: she can no longer work for the community, so she does what she can do to the best of her ability. The artist has touched her with blue to suggest the constancy with which she thought of Mary. This is a painting of prayer, of that simple, absolute surrender to God that gives God freedom to act.

It is painful to read about Bernadette's life in the convent and its harshness. She accepted it all quietly, often subduing her robust peasant spirit so as to accept humbly and gratefully whatever happened. Her death was long and painful, but she clasped the Hail Mary to her heart, with total trust and submission. "Pray for us sinners, now and at the hour of our death." "Us sinners… us sinners" were her last words, because nobody is more aware than a saint of our profound need of God's forgiveness.

St Agatha,
dates unknown but very early

The Martyrdom of St Agatha, by Giambattista Tiepolo (1696–1770), Old Master Museum, Berlin, Germany

When I was about ten, my mother bought the full set of *Butler's Lives of the Saints*. I can see them now, green and gold, in the glass cabinet. I was thrilled at the thought of all these large, holy books to read, but I confess, with shame, that I never got further than the first volume. It was St Agatha who stopped me in my eager tracks. For one just beginning to understand that one passed from childhood into, eventually, womanhood, reading what was done to Agatha aroused a great wave of fear, indignation and grief. Because she would not sacrifice to the pagan gods, the Roman authorities cut off her breasts and she bled to death. I could not bear it, yet bearing what happens in life is the way to God. I sorrowed for a long time over poor, mutilated St Agatha, and the terrible choices that some people are evidently asked to make. Even if I foolishly read no more of *Butler's Lives*, at least I had read enough to make me realise my own softness and weakness, and how very much I had need of the support of prayer.

I wish I had seen Tiepolo's painting of St Agatha in her martyrdom. He disguises none of the pain or horror, but he shows with extraordinary power what this dying girl did with that pain. In the painting she is already almost bloodless. Her face, deathly white, is in striking contrast to the two healthy faces that press in on either side. Neither seems hostile. The pageboy is bearing away the two pathetic mounds of flesh that are her breasts. The pagan priestess helps hold the cloth to her wounds. Both look vaguely interested, but essentially unconcerned. The executioner looms savagely over her, and a prurient bystander peeks at the plate. Agatha is dying without any obvious divine support, she holds out her hands with her fading strength, and lifts her face to heaven, tear-stained with red-rimmed eyes.

Nothing in art to me surpasses that dying look. It always reminds me of that line from the book of Job in the Old Testament: "Though he slay me, yet will I trust in him." Agatha trusts, absolutely. Jesus has not saved her from death and she sees no miraculous signs of his presence. Yet she believes. She knows that through all the humiliation and agony her Lord has been with her, to support and comfort her. The comfort is not in anything she sees or hears, it is not in anything she feels: it is in what she believes. She believes that her life is in God's hands and that her martyrdom will unite her to him.

This seems to me the essence of holiness or, if you like, the essence of our religion: we are all called to live by faith. Whatever happens to us, good or bad, we make use of it, we let it draw us to God. Agatha is praying to be rescued, and her prayer is being answered, though not in the way she would choose. All prayer is answered, and it is answered by God in giving us grace to accept what actually happens. We can see with marvellous clarity (because Tiepolo is a great artist) what is happening to St Agatha, the very thing she is praying to escape. And we can see too, even more marvellously, how God is enabling her to make use of her pain and her death. Her upward gaze never falters. Light shines on her physically, from the left: it shines too on the pillar and the pageboy. But Tiepolo suggests another inner light, a luminescence that irradiates her interiorly. That intensity of faith brings her to heaven, while she is still most painfully on earth. This is what faith offers, here to St Agatha, and now, today, to us.

If I had seen this painting I would not have been frightened all those years ago by St Agatha and her breasts. Or, rather, I would have been frightened, but I would have been able, please God, to unite my fear to that of Jesus in the agony in the garden. Of course we shrink from pain and death. If Jesus did, so will we. But the death of Jesus redeemed the world, and every death, like St Agatha's, can and should be redemptive.

St Serapion, 1179–1240

St Serapion, 1628, by Francisco de Zurbarán
(1598–1664), Wadsworth Athenaeum, Museum of
Art, Hartford, Connecticut, USA

St Serapion, to my surprise, turns out to have been an
Englishman (or possibly an Irishman), Peter Serapion. He
must have been both a devoted and an adventurous young
man because he went to Spain to fight with the armies of
Castile, as King Alfonso IX tried to hold back the Moorish
invasion. While he was there, though, he was very struck
by the work of the Mercedarians, a religious order that was
especially established to care for those who were captured by
the Muslims. Since many of these captives were tempted to
buy their freedom by renouncing their faith, the Mercedarians
tried to ransom them or, if that failed, to offer themselves in
their place.

Serapion could see that this was the extreme expression of
Christian love, giving your life for another. He joined the
order in 1222, when he was already a mature soldier, and
laboured hard to make people understand the necessity and the
greatness of this practical expression of Christian charity. I will
not go into the grisly details of his death, but they included
being bound hand and foot to two poles.

Zurbarán was among the greatest of artists, with a peculiarly Spanish *gravitas* and power. Although he was relatively young when he painted this work, he never surpassed it, and nor has any other artist. It was painted for the Mercedarian monastery in Seville, to hang in the mortuary chapel where monks lay in state, awaiting their funeral Mass. This detail is only of importance because it explains why St Serapion is shown, as it were, asleep. His brethren, "asleep in the Lord", would lie beneath this painting. It was a gory and horrific death and he is still hanging from the poles to which he was bound, rather as Jesus hangs from the cross. Yet, and this is the great visual glory of the painting, his thick, white, religious habit is spotless. It is as if, like the monks laid out in the chapel, he has been washed and reclad in full monastic dignity. Even his face, eyes closed, shows none of the trauma of his anguish.

We know little about Peter Serapion except that he gave himself to a work of charity that he thought was important, and was steadfast to death. But those great swags of thick white cloth, on which light and shade both play, suggest the subliminal purity of such a life. He gave himself to love; love cleanses and sanctifies him. The garment seems symbolic of the man. A vocation truly understood and embraced bears us up within itself.

Few of us will be called to lead a life dedicated to so heroic a purpose as that of the Mercedarians. Thank God we no longer need an order whose members will sell themselves into slavery to ransom others! But to some extent being a mercedarian, with a small "m", is part of the Christian faith. Jesus repeated, again and again, how essential it is that we should serve one another, that our love should be self-sacrificing and practical. For some people every day offers opportunities for many mini-martyrdoms: small surrenders of their own freedom for the sake of others. These sacrifices have no apparent grandeur about them, and we know that, in actuality, St Serapion's sacrifice would have been the absolute opposite of grand or sublime. It would have been horrible, completely without dignity, dirty and bloody.

Zurbarán shows us not the facts but the truth, and, in the calm amplitude in which the dying saint stretches out his arms in death, we have an image of that sacrificial surrender that Our Lord asks of us, in our ordinary lives. Zurbarán makes it clear that this is not meant to be a literal painting, by imitating, on the right side, a label with his signature.

The whites and the blacks, the light and the dark, the monumental stillness of this work are an implicit celebration of sacrificial holiness.

St Helena,
c. 250–330

The Vision of St Helena, c. 1560–1565, by Paolo
Veronese (1528–1588), National Gallery, London

We tend to be amused and scornful about the medieval passion
for relics: the slivers of the True Cross that could be rebuilt into
a forest, the phial of the milk of the Virgin, the hair from the
beard of John the Baptist, even a feather from the wing of the
angel Gabriel. Of course, these so-called relics have utterly no
religious value in themselves, yet they do represent a longing
to be closer to the holy. Let us at least be willing to admit that
the desire behind them is not unworthy.

The True Cross, which was so profoundly venerated in
the Middle Ages and which was the focus of such genuine
religious emotion, owed its existence to St Helena. Part of
the prestige of this relic came from Helena's status. She was
the mother of Constantine the Great, the emperor who first
prescribed tolerance of the Christian faith throughout the
Roman empire. Constantine, despite his religious enthusiasm,
was only baptised on his deathbed, the rationale being that
he could go straight from baptism to heaven. His mother,

though, seems to have been a believer for some time, and she became possessed of a great desire to visit the Holy Land and worship Our Lord in the places where he suffered.

Despite her wealth and position, such a pilgrimage would have been both arduous and hazardous. When she set out, sometime after 313, she was already in her sixties, a great age for the times, though years of travelling around with her soldier husband had probably toughened her. She came into Palestine with money, influence and great spiritual longing: we can hardly be surprised that the "holy places" were pointed out to her, and the "True Cross" eventually discovered.

Legend has it that while she was sleeping she had a vision of the True Cross carried by angels, and this is what Veronese shows us. His Helena is not a battered old warhorse (that was not Veronese's style), but an elegant and sensuous beauty, reclining gracefully at a window in her palace. Having seen the cross, she was of course able to distinguish it from false crosses. In other words, she knew in advance that she was called to find the cross, and that she would find it – which could in fact be a recipe for delusion. Yet is this not what we all would desire? If we were to have a vision, we think, if we were to know for certain what we were meant to do or to become, how simply and happily we could respond to God's will.

But, as we know, God does not generally send us the sweet clarity of visions. We have to stumble around, praying and searching, usually quite uncertain as to whether we are doing what God wants. We envy those – and they certainly exist – who have this certainty, even when it does not come from visionary experience. Our ignorance leaves us pitifully vulnerable. But this is precisely how we grow in closeness to Our Lord. Our ignorance forces us to recognise our need of him, and our need forces us to turn to him in prayer. He never asks for the "right decision", only the decision that, after prayer and reflection, seems to us to be right.

Looking back over the centuries, we can see that all St Helena suffered to come close to Our Blessed Lord through his cross did bring her close to him. Whatever the truth of what she discovered, God looked at her eagerness and faith. She used the True Cross as a means of prayer, and moved through it to the Lord who she thought hung upon it. She found him, and in him that blessed end that we all seek.

St Thomas Aquinas, 1225–1274

St Thomas Aquinas, 1476, by Carlo Crivelli
(c. 1435–1495), National Gallery, London

There seem to have been quite a few clever saints (St Augustine,
St Teresa of Ávila) and the occasional genius (St Francis and,
to my mind, St Thérèse of Lisieux). But St Thomas Aquinas is
in a class of his own. Intellectually, he dominated the Middle
Ages, the great "angelic doctor" – "doctor", remember,
meaning "teacher". He taught the Church in his own day
and he teaches it still. His *Summa Theologica* may no longer
be the only source of the Church's theology, but it remains
an extraordinary achievement and will always reward study.
Crivelli shows St Thomas as holding his teaching in one hand,
while in the other he clasps to himself the beloved Church.
Between the book and the Church we can see an image of the
sun: he was an essential light-bringer.

What St Thomas did for the Church, with the finesse, clarity
and authority that no theologian has ever equalled, was to
bring order to the complexities of religious speculation. He
drew out the meanings of the Gospels and St Paul, while

simultaneously exploring the powerful and often daunting rationality of Aristotle. He showed how faith could not but be both in accord with reason and above it, though never at odds with it. One is still awed by the vastness of his mental capacity, and the simplicity with which he could strip the most abstruse doctrine down to its fundamentals, analyse it and show its relationship to the whole body of faith.

Artists tend to show this great scholar as an ascetic figure, worn out by his constant nightly vigils. Crivelli has the truth of it, or, rather, is more truthful than most. His Thomas is a burly figure with a large, good-humoured face. The real Thomas was immensely fat. This may well have been the result of a metabolic disorder, yet in this age of obesity it is a comfort to think that at least one saint experienced for himself the painful burden of too much flesh. Poor St Thomas actually had to have a semicircle cut out of the table in the friars' refectory so that he could get within touching distance of the meagre Dominican fare.

He joined the Dominicans against parental opposition. The family were aristocrats who wanted him to be a lordly Benedictine abbot. High-born or not, he was, apparently, a large, shambling, shy young man with a ready smile and slow speech. The other novices called him "the dumb ox", and his teacher, St Albert, another great Dominican scholar, told them in reproof that the bellowings of this "dumb ox" would enlighten the world. Despite his unromantic appearance, Thomas was a true poet. The *O Salutaris Hostia* and the *Tantum Ergo*, which we sing in honour of the Blessed Sacrament, were written by St Thomas.

> "Faith will tell us Christ is present,
> when our human senses fail."

His faith was intense. At the end of his life, though he was still in his forties, a youngish man, he said that he could write about God no more. All that he had written, he said, "seemed like straw".

St Dorothy,
died c. 300

St Dorothy and the Infant Christ, c. 1460s, by an
associate of Francesco di Giorgio (1439–1501),
National Gallery, London

St Dorothy is not one of the popular female saints like St Mary
Magdalene or St Catherine, but the National Gallery has two
very different depictions of her. The more famous is by the
Master of the St Bartholomew Altarpiece. This Dorothy is a
pert, curvaceous young woman in a skintight robe of the most
fetching elegance. Delightful creature though she is, I cannot
warm to this reading of the saint's character. The unknown
artist who painted the small image here of *St Dorothy and the
Infant Christ* has never achieved more recognition than that
of being associated with the better-known (yet still not a
household name) Francesco di Giorgio. What it lacks in artistic
skills is supplied by a touching innocence. This seems to me
highly appropriate for Dorothy, who is one of the sweetest-
natured among the saints.

According to the legend, she refused to sacrifice to the
pagan gods, and was condemned to execution. As she was
led through the city to her death, she passed a young lawyer

called Theophilus. Apparently he was struck by her look of radiant expectation: Dorothy knew that she was on the point of seeing for herself the face of Jesus. What he saw as this foolish expression of hope infuriated Theophilus. He began to expostulate with the silly girl who, after all, could still change her mind, sprinkle the incense and lead a normal and happy life. Dorothy listened graciously to his contemptuous outburst, a cruel interruption on her way to paradise, and assured him that she knew what she was doing. He shouted after her that she should send him fruit and flowers when she got to heaven. He stalked off, she moved peacefully on, the executioner did his duty. Almost immediately a small child – this artist thinks it was the Christ child, others have thought it an angel – came up to Theophilus and gave him a basket of roses and apples. Since it was winter, he had no option but to see this as a gentle response to his jeering request. We may not be surprised to learn that St Theophilus the Lawyer himself died a martyr for the faith.

This little St Dorothy, with her English-rose complexion and her neat waves of golden hair, her beautiful but modest garments and her air of gentle trustfulness, seems to make visual the Christian meaning of the story. A Christian is one who always treats the other with respect. Dorothy had every reason to feel hurt by the sneers of Theophilus, but she responded with a quiet humour. He asked for the impossible, fruit and flowers in winter, and she was able to prove to him that "with God all things are possible".

The little Jesus who is holding the miraculous basket looks like Dorothy's young brother. Incidentally, there are only roses in the basket – perhaps the artist was not up to painting both flowers and fruit. Dorothy holds the child Jesus with the quiet familiarity of one who has known him for many years in prayer. She looks down at her Lord with the same affectionate reverence as she must have looked up at the angry lawyer. After all, for those who love Our Lord, everyone is Our Lord. Everyone is to be treated with the love that we would offer Jesus in person. Our faith asks us to take others seriously, to listen to them, to try to help them in so far as is possible. Dorothy treated Theophilus in the same way as she would have wanted Christ to treat her.

Because the picture is so small it was probably painted for private devotion. I like to think of some medieval Italian family kneeling before this picture, and understanding through it the implications of Christian charity.

St Catherine of Alexandria, c. 282 – c. 305

St Catherine of Alexandria, probably 1515–1530, attributed to Garofalo (1481–1559), National Gallery, London

There are at least sixteen St Catherines. All are named after the original St Catherine, who was one of the most popular of saints throughout the Middle Ages and beyond. Yet, like St Christopher, there is little evidence of her existence. There is an interesting philosophical point here: when is a saint not a saint? The thought of St Christopher protecting travellers has comforted many enduring a long and perhaps dangerous journey. The thought of St Catherine, valiant in defence of her faith, beautiful and wholehearted in her devotion, has inspired Christians throughout the centuries. Artists have loved to depict both these saints. One wonders why they were held so tenaciously in Christian memory if there was no substratum, however small, of reality. St Catherine is part of our religious history, and teaches us something about the nature of holiness.

One can see why some have rather baulked at the melodramatics of her legend. She was apparently a young woman of astonishing beauty, highly born, sought in marriage by the Roman emperor himself (in some versions the emperor's son). She refused him, citing her Christianity. The lovelorn emperor sent fifty pagan philosophers to remonstrate with her; Catherine converted the lot of them, whereupon the furious emperor slaughtered the fifty new Christians, and condemned Catherine to death upon the wheel. It was a wheel with knives attached to it (I am not quite sure of the mechanics) and as it turned it was designed to slice its victims to death. When Catherine was bound to the wheel, it burst free, bounded across the execution yard and killed the wicked spectators. Gnashing his teeth, the emperor had her put to death by the infallible sword.

The wheel is the emblem in art of St Catherine, and its appealing shape, that lovely rotundity, may be one of the reasons why artists have always been attracted to her. Raphael painted one of the most wonderful St Catherines, all curves and amplitudes, as rounded in herself as the wheel on which she leans. Garofalo is a relatively minor artist and this is not even positively one of his works: it is only "attributed". But I like it for its seriousness. You can just see the wheel at the bottom left corner. She holds the palm branch of martyrdom and caresses it gently. The legend holds her to be a great scholar, able to argue down fifty learned pagans. There is something about this young woman, with her broad brow and widely spaced eyes, that conveys the thoughtfulness and earnestness that alone make fruitful any explanation of the faith.

It is not enough to know our religion intellectually, to be able to write articles or even books about it. What matters is to live it. We are called to a genuine relationship with Our Blessed Lord, and, in him, with the Father and the Holy Spirit. We enter this relationship at baptism and we grow in it through prayer, and the necessary sign of our prayer is goodness. Goodness is a very wide and vague expression, yet we all know what it means. If we are not "good", eager to be good, then we are not praying. If we are praying, then the inevitable result will be this practical expression of love that we call goodness. I think that the legendary story of St Catherine converting the philosophers is a dramatic expression of this. Their words came from their intellect alone; hers came from an intellect, a loving intellect, suffused with the grace of God.

I am also intrigued by the miracle of the wheel. We have a contemporary distaste for explosions, but it is from St Catherine that the firework the Catherine wheel takes its name. It was a splendid miracle that saved her, yet what is its real significance? The wheel bursts, Catherine survives, the executioner takes a sword and finishes her. Does it not suggest strongly that earthly miracles are just that, earthly, and that we Christians have our eyes fixed on what is non-earthly and eternal?

St Jerome, c. 347–420

St Jerome in a Rocky Landscape, c. 1515–1524,
attributed to Joachim Patenier (c. 1480–1524),
National Gallery, London

For some reason, artists have always been enthusiastic about
St Jerome. He appears in two completely different settings,
each of which pays tribute to one side of his complex nature.
He is most famous today as a scholar: the pertinacious traveller
in the Holy Land, teaching himself Hebrew, exploring Greek
literature, and finally accepting a commission to translate the
entire Bible and comment on it. This life of dedicated scholarly
activity intrigued artists, who loved to imagine the details of
his study, with its shelves of books and all the contemporary
apparatus of scholarship.

Yet St Jerome was no dry-as-dust scholar. He was a passionate
seeker after Christ, at intervals throwing aside his dictionaries
and retreating into the desert to pray. There he agonised
over his sinfulness, and many artists show him beating his
breast with a stone or prostrate before a crucifix. Somewhere
in both scenes will usually be the scarlet of a cardinal's hat,

although in fact there were no cardinals in the time of Jerome. Nevertheless, he somehow seemed to artists a natural cardinal, a virtual wearer of the scarlet.

Also in the picture is usually a lion. When St Jerome was living as a monk, he removed a thorn from a lion's paw, and the grateful beast became attached to the monastery. When thieves stole the monastic donkey, the monks blamed the lion, despite St Jerome's passionate protests. The heartbroken animal pursued the thieves until he could bring back in triumph the missing donkey, a triumph in which St Jerome fully shared (moral: do not be quick to judge).

Unfortunately there is written evidence to show that St Jerome's tenderness seems to have extended only to lions and holy women. He was a ferocious and bad-tempered correspondent, a profoundly argumentative man who could not brook disagreement. No wonder artists depict him beating his breast in contrition: he had much about which to be contrite! Yet the passion that soured his human intellectual contacts was the same passion that was at the heart of his immense desire to love God. His years in the wilderness were precious to him, and he returned constantly either to absolute solitude or to the comparative solitude of a monastery.

This painting, typical of the artist Joachim Patenier in its sweeping bird's-eye view of the world, shows St Jerome, small and humble, in the foreground. His companion is the faithful lion. He is clearly there to pray and to repent, possibly to repent of his bad temper and his longing for intellectual stimulation.

Intense as he was by temperament, he had times of fearing that he could not afford to enjoy literature and still give himself totally to God. The sharp and towering rocks that surround him are probably symbols of his intense and aspiring nature. In the distance can be seen the monastery and the repentant thieves, but St Jerome has withdrawn from even the most worthy of earthly activities. Patenier suggests that the essential Jerome is not the scholar but the man of God.

St Cecilia,
second to third century

St Cecilia, 1620–1625, by Pietro da Cortona
(1596–1669), National Gallery, London

There are quite a few virgin martyrs from the first centuries, and artists, throwing probability loftily aside, depict all of them as young and beautiful. So that we can distinguish one from another, each has in the course of time acquired an emblem or symbol. These attributes are usually taken from the account of their martyrdom: for example, St Catherine has the wheel that was supposed to tear her to pieces, St Apollonia has the forceps that violently drew out all her teeth, St Margaret has the dragon that swallowed her (until she forced her way out with a crucifix), St Barbara has the tower in which she was imprisoned. St Cecilia is a little different. She is the patron saint of music and her emblem is the portable organ, as well as whatever other musical instruments strike the artist's fancy.

Pietro da Cortona shows her holding the palm of martyrdom in one hand, while in the other she holds pages of manuscript: hymns? Behind her, within easy reach, on the left as we look at the picture, is her organ, while on the right an angel looks soulfully up at her, holding a harp. Yet music had nothing to do with her death and, in fact, it is not easy to pinpoint the factors that have so intimately linked her name with music.

Cecilia was a young woman of high patrician birth. The site of her ancestral home is believed to be underneath the ancient church of St Cecilia in Trastevere. As was inevitable with high-born ladies of the time, she was married off against her will, but here she had a great stroke of good fortune. Her bridegroom, a pagan called Valerius, must have been an exceptional young man. When she explained to him her desire to live a life of virginity for the sake of Christ, he accepted her decision. The legend tells us that during the marriage ceremonies she sang to God in her heart, and it may be from this spiritual singing that the belief arose that she was especially musical. Valerius and his brother Tiburtius were so impressed by the strength of her faith that they too became Christians, and were martyred even before the judges came for Cecilia. The story then becomes rather confused, with one account holding that she was suffocated to death by boiling steam in her private bathroom, another that she was merely beheaded. How she died seems much less important than how she lived, and whatever the literal truth of her story the impression left on Christian Rome was that she was one who expressed her love of God through her love of music.

This is more important than it might seem. There appears to be in human nature a fear of pleasure, and the saints are so often shown as those who embrace eagerly penance and mortification. But God comes to us through all the beauty of the world, just as much as in its pain. God is there in sunlight and in summer as much as in storms and in winter. Some people, some saints, have tormented themselves over such things as their love for literature, like St Jerome, or their loathing of cheese, like St Margaret Mary Alacoque. But God is very present in literature, and God is very present in a physical incapacity to digest a food. We need constantly to remind ourselves of God's all-pervading presence, how God wants to come to us at every angle, at every moment, and how we are missing God because we are inattentive or narrow-minded.

It is hard not to be aware of God's divine presence in music. It can lift us out of the limitations of our selfishness, rather in the way that prayer does. If some painting is visual prayer, then music can be aural prayer.

When we respond to the psalm, and "sing and make music to the Lord", we are in communion with St Cecilia.

St John the Baptist, first century

St John the Baptist Retiring to the Desert, c. 1453, by Giovanni di Paolo (c. 1400–1482), National Gallery, London

St John the Baptist is unique among the saints. He belongs as much to the Old Testament as he does to the New: he is a prophet but he is the last of the prophets. His great moment, of course, was when he was called by Jesus to baptise him, and it is naturally that scene that artists most often depict. There are some wonderful paintings of John preaching, but it is John standing in the Jordan with Jesus, reverently baptising him, that is the crucial image. They look so alike: two young men – yet one the Son of God, and the other of whom Jesus said, "of all the children born of women, there is no one greater than John; yet the least in the kingdom of God is greater than he is".

John the Baptist lived in the desert, in conditions of extreme austerity. He wore camel skin with a leather girdle and lived on locusts and wild honey. Giovanni di Paolo is inspired to show us the young John, setting out from his parents' house, with its fancy frontage, and leaving all the comforts of home so that he can live alone with God. It is a very rare depiction of a lovable and even charming John. He is still in his pretty pink garment, and, like all young adventurers, he carries on his shoulder a stick from which hangs a small bag of provisions. This image suggests that he did not anticipate the full rigours of what would be his vocation. He launched himself upon it with a full heart, and it would be in the years ahead that God would unfold to him the true dimensions of his vocation: just like us, in fact.

We think of holiness as a state of closeness to Jesus. That is the longing of every saint, and of every Christian, to be like Jesus. But for most of his life John was compared to Jesus, and not always to his disadvantage. John fitted much more the pattern of what people think of as sanctity, there in the desert "not eating bread, not drinking wine". Jesus lived among his fellow men and women, a much more ordinary life. He ate and drank, went to parties, blessed children and had women followers. The Pharisees, who said of John the Baptist, "he is possessed", called Jesus "a glutton and a drunkard, a friend of tax collectors and sinners".

John saw very little, physically, of Jesus, yet surely he was united to him more profoundly than anyone except Our Lady. We can see how pointless it is to compare their lifestyles, and this holds equally for each of us. No one vocation is "better" than another. The penitential solitary in the desert lost for hours in contemplation may be no closer to God than the busy mother or taxi driver or schoolteacher (fill in your own profession). All God asks is that we respond completely to our own vocation, however ordinary it may seem.

Jesus gloried in the vocation of John. John pondered anxiously over the vocation, the meaning, of Jesus. His was the glory of preparing the way of the Lord, a way he himself was not privileged to travel. We see the fullness of his holiness in his humble acceptance of this.

St Francis of Assisi, c.1181–1226

St Francis Renounces his Earthly Father, 1437–1444, by Sassetta (1392?–1450), National Gallery, London

St Francis is everybody's favourite saint, at least to the extent that everybody has heard of him and responded to him. He seems so unthreatening a saint, "Il Poverello" ("the little poor man"). He is not the only poet among the saints – St John of the Cross is one of the greatest Spanish lyricists – but his is a poetry that is peculiarly childlike and winning. In our environment-conscious age, we delight in a saint who would preach to the birds and to the fish, who could persuade a rogue wolf into virtuous behaviour, and who called the sun his brother and the moon his sister. Francis seems to walk happily through a world in which he sees the goodness of God on every side.

Yet to be little and poor is not merely a poetic concept. Seen in his true dimensions, no saint is more challenging than St Francis. It is true that he was little in body, a small, dark man at whom nobody would look twice, yet whose charisma transfixed all who met him. But the littleness that he sought for himself and his order was the littleness of unimportance. He had known the pleasures of pride in his adolescence, and it was when he saw how self-importance blocked his way to the crucified Jesus that he began to thirst for "littleness" in all its aspects. The world being what it is, a sure way to unimportance is having no money and no possessions. Poverty became central to the Franciscan way of life.

Sassetta painted eight scenes from the life of St Francis for the high altar of a Franciscan church. This one is not one of the more familiar scenes from the saint's life, but it was fundamental. He had been living at home, giving generously to the poor from his future inheritance. But the money actually, of course, still belonged to his father; and when there was domestic anger over this excessive almsgiving, St Francis realised he must live without any security whatever. In a splendid dramatic gesture, he threw off all his clothes, and gave them back to his father. Now he possessed nothing. Symbolically, the bishop, representing the Church, threw a cloak around him.

It makes a good story, yet think of the reality of what Francis had done. From now on he would be dependent on charity. He would beg for his food; he would sleep where he could; he accepted the protection of the Church but only so that he could serve, not so that he could receive.

St Francis was never ordained, not feeling himself worthy of the dignity of being a priest, and he held no position, even though he was the founder of a religious order. His order was to be one of "little brothers" – Friars Minor, unimportant nobodies who went around the towns and villages showing forth the joy of God. He impressed upon them that they must always be preaching, and typically he added that, if they had to, they could even use words. St Francis and his Franciscans, that small band of unimportant men, felt called to preach by what they were.

We know that St Francis bore the wounds of Jesus on his body, but it is more important that he had "the mind of Christ". Jesus clung to no dignity, "he emptied himself", and here we see St Francis trying to "empty" himself, renouncing his family, his lifestyle, and all earthly possessions present and to come.

St George, died c. 300

St George and the Dragon, c. 1470, by Paolo Uccello (c. 1397–1475), National Gallery, London

There seems to be historical certainty that there really was a St George and that he was a martyr in Palestine during the persecution of Diocletian. But at some time his legend attached to itself a dragon, with a whole hinterland of drama. It was an exceptionally voracious dragon, it would seem, blackmailing a city into providing a regular meal of virgins. St George, heroic warrior, arrived in time to save the life of the princess, who then led the dragon captive, using her girdle as a leash.

This may seem mere dramatic embellishment, but in fact St George is the Christian form of a very ancient and widespread human myth. Our remotest ancestors knew to the full, probably even better than we do, how threatening the world is and how helpless we are to protect ourselves. They were certainly more aware than we are of human defencelessness before winter and darkness, flood and famine. But the human heart always hopes for a hero, on a white horse, wearing armour, holding an invincible lance. When evil slithered massively forth from its darkness, the shining knight in his purity and brightness would be there to save us.

Uccello presents us with a gleaming St George and a peculiarly repulsive dragon. In the nastiest of pretences, this great, hideous creature sports decorative rings, as if to lull the suspicions of the powers of virtue. A nice touch is the sedate patience of the little princess, who seems quite unafraid. Not only are St George and his horse thundering to her rescue but behind the saint's head is a strange mass of cloud, suggesting divine intervention. We can see the darkness of the gaping cave of the dragon. That will remain always sealed against the brightness of the sun. Yet what emerges from that darkness, however foul, will be overcome by the powers of goodness.

St George then, real though he is, is not so much a person as a symbol. For the princess and her city, he is a Jesus figure. Their greatest fear and horror is the dragon against which they are helpless, and miraculously a hero comes to their rescue.

But it is a subtle symbol. Not all the work is done by the hero on his horse. He does not actually destroy the dragon, which suggests that the dragon, as a symbol of evil, is essentially indestructible. What he does is to defeat the dragon, then to hand it over to that poignant symbol of frailty, the pale little princess. The saint has wounded the dragon so severely that she, representing us, can tie her girdle around its neck and lead it back to the city, harmless.

It would be more humanly satisfying a legend if we could believe that evil could be wholly removed from our lives. This story indicates that, no, dragons are a constant factor, and so are dark caves. We will not be saved without being prepared to use our girdles and walk back to the city, dragon at our heels. The Christian, who of course has in Jesus the supreme Saviour, can never relax into complacency. Jesus will defeat our dragon whenever we ask him, but it is our dragon, and our responsibility to keep it leashed and helpless.

St Mary Magdalene, first century

Noli Me Tangere, c. 1510–1515, by Titian
(c. 1489–1576), National Gallery, London

Artists have always been attracted to Mary Magdalene. Often they show her in penance, weeping for her sins, for some reason bare to the waist, long hair streaming down her back. Or they show her, beautiful and seductive, holding an alabaster jar of ointment. But this is because they have confused her with two other women in the New Testament: the Mary out of whom Jesus cast seven devils; and the sinful woman who broke a precious alabaster jar of ointment over his feet, when he was dining with Simon the Pharisee. This conflation has no historical validity and, moving though these other depictions are, they cannot reveal to us the Magdalene who spoke to Jesus after the resurrection.

The Gospel of St John brings us very close to this woman. Her heart was broken by the death of Jesus, and all she could find to do to show her love was to prepare his body, wash and clean it, as had not been done after his hurried burial. It comes across very clear to us, her anguish when she finds even this last service is not possible. The tomb is empty: "They have taken away my Lord, and I do not know where they have put him." She means this literally, but many Christians have times when their faith seems dim – they cannot "find Jesus". They must cling to an intellectual certainty that this absence is not objective; it is only emotionally that for them he seems "not present". But for Mary Magdalene, it is fully objective, as she roams the garden on Easter morning, blinded by tears, searching for Jesus.

Whoever searches, finds. Mary Magdalene does indeed find; she meets him, and, as is so often the case with us, she does not recognise him. She thinks he is the gardener, and Titian shows Jesus holding a hoe, which explains her mistake. One of the most moving passages in the whole of scripture is when the so-called gardener turns to her and says, "Mary". She may not recognise him, but Jesus recognises her. He is the one who searches, far more than we do.

We know what happens next. How she drops to her knees, lifted in one moment from the depths of sorrow to the heights of joy. (Perhaps death will be like this for us?) She stretches out her arms to him, and Jesus explains that this is his risen body, not to be touched: to be adored and loved and praised. "Noli me tangere" – "Do not touch me." So, piercing through her ecstatic joy, comes the pain of reality. Like us, she must adore "in spirit and in truth", no longer in body.

You may object that this is a picture of Jesus, rather than of Mary Magdalene, but that is how every saint would choose to be depicted. None of them exists in his or her own right, as it were. All of them take their meaning from the presence in their life of Jesus.

Mary Magdalene had the privilege, of which she was fully aware, of being contemporary with Jesus. Apart from the New Testament saints, all – including ourselves – can only enter this world through prayer. Remember, though, that not everybody who knew Our Lord shared his life. Think of the Pharisees and his other enemies. Our manner of closeness, which depends wholly on faith, can be as transformative for us as physical closeness to Jesus was for Mary Magdalene and the apostles.

If we were to demand a visual representation of what it means to be a saint, this painting might be a good answer. Mary is on her knees looking up to Jesus, absorbed in him, and he holds out a hand in blessing. This is precisely what happens for us, when we pray.